St. Kilda's Parliament

St. Kilda's Parliament

★

DOUGLAS DUNN

FABER AND FABER
London · Boston

First published in 1981
by Faber and Faber Limited
3 Queen Square London WC1N 3AU
Printed in Great Britain by
Latimer Trend & Co Ltd.
All rights reserved

British Library Cataloguing in Publication Data

Dunn, Douglas
St. Kilda's parliament.
I. Title
821'.914   PR6045·U54
ISBN 0-571-11770-8

William Douglas Dunn
1912–1980

Contents

Acknowledgements

Acknowledgements and thanks are due to the editors of the following magazines where some of these poems appeared for the first time: *Akros, Bananas, Encounter, Glasgow Herald, Helix, London Magazine, London Review of Books, Megaphone, New Edinburgh Review, New Statesman, New Yorker, Poetry Review, Poetry Wales, Quarto, Reaper, Seer, Stand, Stone Ferry Review, Thames Poetry, Yale Literary Magazine.*

St. Kilda's Parliament: 1879–1979

The photographer revisits his picture

On either side of a rock-paved lane,
Two files of men are standing barefooted,
Bearded, waistcoated, each with a tam-o'-shanter
On his head, and most with a set half-smile
That comes from their companionship with rock,
With soft mists, with rain, with roaring gales,
And from a diet of solan goose and eggs,
A diet of dulse and sloke and sea-tangle,
And ignorance of what a pig, a bee, a rat,
Or rabbit look like, although they remember
The three apples brought here by a traveller
Five years ago, and have discussed them since.
And there are several dogs doing nothing
Who seem contemptuous of my camera,
And a woman who might not believe it
If she were told of the populous mainland.
A man sits on a bank by the door of his house,
Staring out to sea and at a small craft
Bobbing there, the little boat that brought me here,
Whose carpentry was slowly shaped by waves,
By a history of these northern waters.
Wise men or simpletons—it is hard to tell—
But in that way they almost look alike
You also see how each is individual,
Proud of his shyness and of his small life
On this outcast of the Hebrides
With his eyes full of weather and seabirds,
Fish, and whatever morsel he grows here.
Clear, too, is manhood, and how each man looks
Secure in the love of a woman who

13

Also knows the wisdom of the sun rising,
Of weather in the eyes like landmarks.
Fifty years before depopulation—
Before the boats came at their own request
To ease them from their dying babies—
It was easy, even then, to imagine
St. Kilda return to its naked self,
Its archeology of hazelraw
And footprints stratified beneath the lichen.
See, how simple it all is, these toes
Playfully clutching the edge of a boulder.
It is a remote democracy, where men,
In manacles of place, outstare a sea
That rattles back its manacles of salt,
The moody jailer of the wild Atlantic.

       Traveller, tourist with your mind set on
Romantic Staffas and materials for
Winter conversations, if you should go there,
Landing at sunrise on its difficult shores,
On St. Kilda you will surely hear Gaelic
Spoken softly like a poetry of ghosts
By those who never were contorted by
Hierarchies of cuisine and literacy.
You need only look at the faces of these men
Standing there like everybody's ancestors,
This flick of time I shuttered on a face.
Look at their sly, assuring mockery.
They are aware of what we are up to
With our internal explorations, our
Designs of affluence and education.
They know us so well, and are not jealous,
Whose be-all and end-all was an eternal
Casual husbandry upon a toehold
Of Europe, which, when failing, was not their fault.
You can see they have already prophesied

A day when survivors look across the stern
Of a departing vessel for the last time
At their gannet-shrouded cliffs, and the farewells
Of the St. Kilda mouse and St. Kilda wren
As they fall into the texts of specialists,
Ornithological visitors at the prow
Of a sullenly managed boat from the future.
They pose for ever outside their parliament,
Looking at me, as if they have grown from
Affection scattered across my own eyes.
And it is because of this that I, who took
This photograph in a year of many events—
The Zulu massacres, Tchaikovsky's opera—
Return to tell you this, and that after
My many photographs of distressed cities,
My portraits of successive elegants,
Of the emaciated dead, the lost empires,
Exploded fleets, and of the writhing flesh
Of dead civilians and commercial copulations,
That after so much of that larger franchise
It is to this island that I return.
Here I whittle time, like a dry stick,
From sunrise to sunset, among the groans
And sighings of a tongue I cannot speak,
Outside a parliament, looking at them,
As they, too, must always look at me
Looking through my apparatus at them
Looking. Benevolent, or malign? But who,
At this late stage, could tell, or think it worth it?
For I was there, and am, and I forget.

The Apple Tree

'And if the world should end tomorrow, I still would plant my apple tree.'

Luther

I could play the bad eras like a concertina.
Multiple chords would squeak like 'excuse me',
'I beg your pardon', 'Oops' and 'Sorry, no thank you.'
Pump hard on a squeeze-box and you can almost hear
The Protestant clerks of northern Europe in Hell,
Complaisant men who filed the paperwork of death
Or signed the warrants, exemplary in private life
But puritanical before their desks of duty.
Say what you like, their Gods did not approve of them.

Men moaned of Scotland that its barren air and soil
Couldn't so much as ripen an apple. I can hear
Their croaked whispers reproach the stern and wild of Alba,
Naming our Kirk, our character, our coarse consent
To drunken decency and sober violence,
Our paradox of ways. Here, in the lovely land,
Beside Kirkmaiden, enumerating apple trees,
I feel the simple millions groan, 'Keep you your faith.
A sapling nursed to fruit impersonates salvation.'

Kirk-sanctioned crimes, Kirk-flourished trade, Kirk-coded
                                                 commerce—
Say what you like, our Gods have not approved of them
While apples ripen round the mist-mild farms and gardens.
Good nature and a scent of fruit at dailygone
Make more of our acceptances and affirmations
Than quick links forced from character to climate.
Name you our beasts and trees, our rivers raced with fish,
Our islands, oceans, mountains and our field-sweet crops.
These too define a people named in city stone.

Four horses chew among the windfalls. Fallen fruits
Spill sweetening juices on the orchard grass, frosted
Into their leaking bruises and hoofed into pulp.
Last wasps grow fat and a tantrum of stings threatens
The man on his ladder, who cups an apple in
The stretch of his hand, then plucks it down, to bite
Its greeny red, rubbed on his overalls. He stands
Up there, eating an apple among all the apples
While big mares and their foals munch on the apple-grass.

At night the orchard is a brew of leaf and fruit,
Feeling the pinch of autumn. Spread sneddins release
The sounds that lie in wait in wood, and over there
An upland wilderness reposes in chilled beauty.
Burns spate with cleanliness of rain, that clean high ground
Of carrion crow and the left-alone mountain sheep.
Crag-country, wet and wiry, but fertile to the eye;
A lung-and-heart testing land, but by a ruin there
You will find crab-apple trees, black harp-strings in the wind.

Tonight I saw the stars trapped underneath the water.
I signed the simple covenant we keep with love.
One hand held out an apple while the other held
Earth from a kirkyard where the dead remember me.
In these lost hollows of the stern conventicles
A faith is kept with land and fruit. Already are
New scriptures written by the late-arriving autumn,
That postponed shuffle of leaves, that white frost-writing.
These are my missionary fruits, a kindred taste.

Then let my Gods be miracles brought on stone boats
By Conval and the first dailyday folk before him.
Rather an ordinary joy—a girl with a basket,
With apples under a linen cloth—than comfortless
With whindlestrae to eat. Forge no false links of man
To land or creed, the true are good enough. Our lives
Crave codes of courtesy, ways of describing love,
And these, in a good-natured land, are ways to weep,
True comfort as you wipe your eyes and try to live.

An Address on the Destitution
of Scotland

Who would have thought it, and not me, not me,
That a boy who shawed turnips with a large gully
By the side of Cousar's cart and snort-breathed Clydesdale,
Who worked in the blue-and-red darkening dusk of childhood,
Would grow into this archivist of Red desires?
Far away are the chills of original Octobers.
My eyes are heavy now with alien perspectives,
And I am sick of the decisions of philosophers—
Dirty hands, dirty hands of turncoats and opinion-makers.
It was a long road back to this undeclared Republic.
I came by the bye-ways, empty of milestones,
On the roads of old drovers, by disused workings.

So here I am, returned to your shabby encampments.
I, too, have scrounged on open fields, ripped up
Into their gathering of released good stinks
That mingle in the first-few-hours-of-shaws-rotting,
That reek of roots, that tactile, lunatic aroma
Tasting of dialect and curses sent out to work.
Tell me of your tinkerdom, of this poverty
Among you, raddled by a destitute polity,
The fields abandoned to old supermarket trolleys,
An ancient soot, the Clyde returning to its nature.
On which blasphemy do you blame your outcast silence,
Bedraggled here with your billy-cans and supper?

Share with me, then, the sad glugs in your bottles;
Throw a stolen spud for me on the side-embers.
Allow me to pull up a brick, and to sit beside you
In this nocturne of modernity, to speak of the dead,
Of the creatures loping from their dens of extinction.
Who are you waiting for? The stern mountain-preacher
In his coat of biblical night? I have seen him.
He sleeps in a kiln, out of the way of dragoons;
And I met a subversive optimist, at Sanquhar.
Permit me, then, to join your circle around your fire
In this midden of warm faces and freezing backs.
Sing me your songs in the speech of timber and horse.

Dominies

White is the January, and schoolboys' scuffed
Footprints in the snow lead to the sound of a bell.
It is Scotland and I attend the dead dominies.
A hand is spinning the globe, saying 'Galileo'
In a cold classroom, in a puff of chalk-dust.
Dominies, dead now, forgive these gauche lines,
My compromised parsings. Boyhood's grammarians
Set down the long examination, 'ink exercises'
At moments of mania, running riot through
The iron language like a trill of angry Rs.
'What sorts of men were the Caesars? Did you heave an axe,
At the wall, against them? Did you stand for your country?
Keep up with the translation. It is good for you.
Horace. Livy. Ballantyne. I am already historical.'

Witch-girl

For evermore, they said, that girl was lame
In hands and feet, and that, they said, was proof
The lightless Devil spelled her into horse,
Moulding her hands and feet in solid hoof.

Poor girl, her mother saddled her, then rode
Through Sutherland until the outraged Law
Attended to the giddy-ups of gossip,
Force-feeding both of them on Tolbooth straw.

Only her mother was condemned. A pious mob—
Citizens and presbyters—whinnied, neighed,
Clip-clopped, as, standing in their fear of God,
There too were men who watched but also pitied.

Cold day in Dornoch . . . Shivering, the witch
Relieved her freezing round that fire which burned
To burn her up. Crowds psalmed with horror.
She blistered in the tar and, screaming, burned.

They spoke in Dornoch how the horses mourned
And how that lame girl, wandering, was heard
Tearing at the grass; and how she sat and sang,
As if the Devil also made her bird;

And how she washed her lameness in the rivers
From Oykell to the Clyde and Tweed and Forth,
Notorious as something to be pitied,
A girl to look at but a beast in worth.

No one could see her but would think he saw
Hoof in her fumbling hands, her staggering gait.
They spurned her flowers, as if they'd grown from her;
They barbed their righteous charity with hate.

She hawked her flowers in Glasgow, by the Trongate;
In Edinburgh, selling flowers, she slept
Beside the braziers of the City Guard.
The earth and animals within her wept.

No one to help her; no one saw her die,
If she is dead. By Gryfe, by Deveron,
By Cree and Tay, I see her wash her lameness,
And hear her breathing in the wood and stone.

Washing the Coins

You'd start at seven, and then you'd bend your back
Until they let you stand up straight, your hands
Pressed on your kidneys as you groaned for lunch,
Thick sandwiches in grease-proofed bundles, piled
Beside the jackets by the hawthorn hedges.
And then you'd bend your little back again
Until they let you stand up straight. Your hands,
On which the earth had dried in layers, itched, itched,
Though worse still was that ache along the tips
Of every picking finger, each broken nail
That scraped the ground for sprawled potatoes
The turning digger churned out of the drills.
Muttering strong Irish men and women worked
Quicker than local boys. You had to watch them.
They had the trick of sideways-bolted spuds
Fast to your ear, and the upset wire basket
That broke your heart but made the Irish laugh.
You moaned, complained, and learned the rules of work.
Your boots, enlarging as the day wore on,
Were weighted by the magnets of the earth,
And rain in the face was also to have
Something in common with bedraggled Irish.
You held your hands into the rain, then watched
Brown water drip along your chilling fingers
Until you saw the colour of your skin
Through rips disfiguring your gloves of mud.
It was the same for everyone. All day
That bead of sweat tickled your smeared nose
And a glance upwards would show you trees and clouds
In turbulent collusions of the sky

With ground and ground with sky, and you portrayed
Among the wretched of the native earth.
Towards the end you felt you understood
The happy rancour of the Irish howkers.
When dusk came down, you stood beside the byre
For the farmer's wife to pay the labour off.
And this is what I remember by the dark
Whitewash of the byre wall among shuffling boots.
She knew me, but she couldn't tell my face
From an Irish boy's, and she apologized
And roughed my hair as into my cupped hands
She poured a dozen pennies of the realm
And placed two florins there, then cupped her hands
Around my hands, like praying together.
It is not good to feel you have no future.
My clotted hands turned coins to muddy copper.
I tumbled all my coins upon our table.
My mother ran a basin of hot water.
We bathed my wages and we scrubbed them clean.
Once all that sediment was washed away,
That residue of field caked on my money,
I filled the basin to its brim with cold;
And when the water settled I could see
Two English kings among their drowned Britannias.

Galloway Motor Farm

They spoil a farm, already written off
Against experience or income tax—
Two Land Rovers, several tractors,
These wooden cattle-floats like shanty huts;
A Jaguar, garaged in the air and grass,
On highways of self-heal and lady's bedstraw;
A Morris shooting-brake is bedded down
With agricultural gear and tackle.

Scattered beside derelict byres and barns,
Awkward, out of place, they lie here, eyesores
Cast out from progress, maladroitly banned
Machinery, discarded implements.
Wastrel existences, I can hear them
As each one wrestles free of function,
Picked over, plundered by who dumped them here,
Already scavenged for their feus of scrap.

The chemistry of weather has installed
Its scaffolding, from which it builds its rusts
On the iron of a horse-drawn reaper.
Air braces itself before stinging nettles.
Car doors, bumpers, bonnets, mudguards, engines—
Earth will not have them back until their steels,
Their chromes, veneers and leathers marry with
These stony contours as the brides of place.

I will be glad to have been here, living
Within this stung bubble where antiquities
Freshen, where they breathe the present tense.
Docken, yarrow, the muscular turf, ignore
These rubbished profits and spent wages.
It all means less than nothing to the bat
On his manic itinerary, and the fox
Was born too late to live with other landmarks.

As for a man, then he may walk beside
These thumbed-down vehicles, posing the moon
Against the window of a truck's high cabin;
Or sit inside, behind the wheel, thinking
A roadless countryside as he pretends
He's motoring through the night. Scotland, come back
From the lost ground of your dismantled lands.
A carelessness has defaced even the bluebell.

Tonight, by a steading, an iron reaper
That once outscythed the scythe
Is a silent cry of its materials,
With all its blunt blades yearning for the stone.
It has come from the yonside of invention,
From pulverable ore and foundry hammers.
Old harness rots above the rusted horseshoes.
Unborn horses graze on the back pastures.

Monumental Sculptor

That look on his face, consulting
His telephone directory,
Is a respectful smirk,
A shading of his dusty eyebrows.

Stooped round his left-hand grip
On a chisel, he is there to tell us
His hammered catalogue of names
Is the stone book of his town.

With lean, ridged muscles of
A man who works with stone,
He sculpts his alphabets
Of memory and consolation.

Notice the slow certainty
Of how his two apprentices
Come round to his likeness,
Inheriting his cut languages.

In the hut of his office
Are spiked invoices and a Bible.
He is in the fashion of God
In that black jacket he wears

When his customers call,
Holding his price-lists and designs,
Discussing the choice of words.
A kettle boils among the stone-dust.

I hear his phone ringing,
As, with a genuflecting crane,
Which squeaks of chains, of stretched links,
They hoist a finished page of marble.

There is no need to answer it,
Not in this trade. The name
Will still be there tomorrow
For his craft of the Kirk's loved ones.

The Harp of Renfrewshire

Contemplating a map

Annals of the trilled R, gently stroked L,
Lamenting O of local literature,
Open, on this, their one-page book, a still
Land-language chattered in a river's burr.

Small-talk of herdsmen, rural argument—
These soft disputes drift over river-meadows,
A darg of conversations, a verbal scent—
Tut-tutted discourse, time of day, word-brose.

Named places have been dictionaried in
Ground's secret lexicon, its racial moan
Of etymology and cries of pain
That slit a summer wind and then were gone.

A mother calls her daughter from her door.
Her house, my stone illusion, hugs its hill.
From Eaglesham west to the rocky shore
Her cry is stretched across bog-asphodel.

The patronymic miles of grass and weddings,
Their festivals of gender, covenants,
Poor pre-industrially scattered steadings,
Ploughed-up davochs—old names, inhabitants.

And on my map is neither wall or fence,
But men and women and their revenue,
As, watching them, I utter into silence
A granary of whispers rinsed in dew.

War Blinded

For more than sixty years he has been blind
Behind that wall, these trees, with terrible
Longevity wheeled in the sun and wind
On pathways of the soldiers' hospital.

For half that time his story's troubled me—
That showroom by the ferry, where I saw
His basketwork, a touch-turned filigree
His fingers coaxed from charitable straw;

Or how he felt when young, enlisting at
Recruiting tables on the football pitch,
To end up slumped across a parapet,
His eye-blood running in a molten ditch;

Or how the light looked when I saw two men,
One blind, one in a wheelchair, in that park,
Their dignity, which I have not forgotten,
Which helps me struggle with this lesser dark.

That war's too old for me to understand
How he might think, nursed now in wards of want,
Remembering that day when his right hand
Gripped on the shoulder of the man in front.

Savings

She saved her money
And she hid her money in
An oriental tin
That came from Twining's Tea.
—'Oh, how much money have you now?'
But she'd never let me see.
She'd place that tin into my hands,
Then with her hands on mine
She'd help me shake her Twining's tin—
Half-crowns and a sovereign,
Shillings, sixpences and florins
Rattled on the paper notes.
That was her funeral fund
I was too young to understand.
When I did, and she was dead,
It wasn't death that I could see
In tea-leaves sifting from a spoon
That came out of a Chinese tin.
I saw the life she'd shovelled in.

Spinster's Wake

I'll look the way I used to be
In my brother's head, when he comes home
To this, my final scullery,
Its curtains drawn to tick and hum
In clock and electricity.
In his new accent, he'll speak of me
As he leans against the mantelpiece
With one ear listening to my clock,
And speak of me, who had no increase.
House with a door, door with a knock,
I lie in a box when my brother comes home
And I'm fresh-dressed and clean and overcome.
Come on in, John, and look at me,
Laid out in my pinny and shawl.
Remember the shelf where I keep the tea,
And your bed in the hole i' the wall?
Pease-brose in the bag, John, jam in the jar,
And day after day on the calendar.
There's a stick in the hall when you take a walk
And your letters are packed behind the clock.
The pot's on the grate, your dram's in the cupboard,
And, Johnny, spare your sister a word
Before there's a knock on her coffin's door
And she goes off to sweep God's kitchen floor.

Rose

So, little rose, it is all over
And you need no longer
Explore your cupped shapes,
Your fine organic enamels.

Four days you sat there
In a simple blue glass.
I watched you, I watched you;
I kept my eye on you.

My love is four days gone from me.
You have been good company.
I knew it would be like this—
You'd die the day of her return.

You have sat there in silence
Like a thought prayer.
You have been my good intentions.
You listened to me with patience.

Now I am in a gentle panic,
Not knowing what to do with you.
I will make up a ritual
For the departures of roses.

You will go into the heaven
Of unforgotten things.
Matisse will paint you;
Or Samuel Peploe will.

The door of her taxi is closing.
But you did not tell me your secrets.
I shall drink the water
Which did not preserve you long enough.

I will remember you in the French language.
I eat you now to keep you for ever.
Hello, my love. See?
This thorn has cut my lips.

Saturday

For Sandra and Chetwyn

Driving along the B1248
We pass such villages as Wetwang, or
North Grimston of descending Z-bends.
The Wolds are rolling for our benefit;
The long woods stride towards the eastern shore.
Frost sparks refrigerated ploughland to
A fan of silver ribs, good husbandry
In straight lines, going downhill to a point,
A misted earthen star, half-frost, half-ground.
And we are going to our country friends
At Kirkbymoorside, bearing a pineapple,
Some books of interest and a fine Bordeaux.
I wish it to be today, always, one hour
On this, the pleasant side of history.

Courting

On a summer's night to come
We'll find ourselves walking
Through a familiar Park.
I feel it happening—
Surprised anachronisms
In a delight, posed as
Hand-holding listeners to
Light overtures, percussed
From a lanterned bandstand
Through shaken foliage.

An autumn afternoon
Rehearses mist and brown
For a rediscovery—
That colour of angels
Flighted with chestnut leaves
Above the arrogant
Scarf-tightening waterfall,
A down-roar of water
Into the sinister
Conventional shadows.

It is already chosen,
A retrospective Sunday
When the still lake is glazed,
When bird-bread breaks underfoot,
Frost-toasted on cinder paths
And rhododendrons look
Snowed green exotica,

A botany of drips:
We will walk there again
With our white conversations.

Gardened from countryside,
The Park heaps love-days
On nature's edge; it is
An album of the Spring
In that season: woodland's
Municipal surprise,
Vernal formalities,
Mute orchestras of bluebells
When light leans on the leaf
And the thrush sings of rain.

Come with me now, dear girl,
And we will walk our years
Together. They open,
As gates do, or books, the heart's
Preliminary landmarks—
That path that leads nowhere
And a meadow beyond;
This path that leads into
Wilder greens of love,
A grass for walking on.

E. A. Walton thinks of painting 'The Daydream'

I kissed my sweet girl-cousins
One by one
Then they grew up
And I never saw them again.
They are lost among
Marriages and houses
At places where
The farms run out of fields
And towns begin.
I remember a girl
Who looked at her own future,
Lying among the flowers—
Milk-pail and butter-churn,
A belled cow led home
On a frayed halter.

The Local

Come, let us lower the tone, talking in
These smoky cadences and lounge-bar whispers.
We will enumerate the lost realia.
The Spirit of the Age will turn its back
And run away from such a narrative.
Notice how beer-mats slip a little on
These inconspicuous pools of slop and spillage.
It suggests half an epiphany is happening.
Or what else is it, tilting in my head,
Which makes me watch the sandwiches grow stale,
That slow bending of bread in perspex bins
At the end of the bar? That, too, explains
A revolution or a crazed malaise
In the wink of a listening stranger.
I can hear music in the oiled hinges
When that door opens, a memory of
Unwritten Mozart or a lost Haydn
In the old man whistling in the Gents
Among the cisterns. Matisse emerges from
A doodled beer-mat; a fingernail engraves
An odalisque from a remembered girl
In a wet bar-counter's puddled drainage.
A man stands muttering his faulty tales
Of Burma in the last days of its Raj.
His eyes glint like a kukri in his dark
Leaf-hidden forays. 'Arakan,' he says,
To no one. 'Rajput. Frightened. Subahdar.'
The Empire ends here, in his anecdotes.
Now add to this the humming of an unplayed
Juke-box. Add chattering at corner tables.

You can hear what I mean in the whirred blades
Of the ventilator's recitations.
Its draughty epic is a literature
Depicting murky ale and tragic drunks
Who were lovers and heroes once, in days
No longer as these ones we live now among
Susurrations and vague moral endeavour.
I shall ingratiate myself with God,
Sticking it out in the land of the living.
Placebo Domino in regione vivorum.
The juke-box hammers out its antiphon.
They service it by feeding in new anthems.
And someone sings, a would-be dandy with
A withered buttonhole. My brain opens.
The streets are bathed in summer and a man
Who's five pence short of what a refill costs
Rejects the dandy's overstated affluence.
We could commune with our ancestors,
Whoever they were. We could talk of life
And death and poetry. We could be neutral,
Smiling with goodwill. Instead, we stand
In this armpit of English vernacular,
Hopelessly in touch with where we are.
The dead lie under our feet like pipelines.
The unacknowledged, counting pennies from
An outstretched palm, know what compassion's worth,
Here, humbly, off a High Street in the North.

Second-hand Clothes

A girl anoints a dress
With four silver coins.
Hands rinse among textiles,
Encountering others' skins.
Held up, observed for rips,
For their proximities
To new, to cleanliness,
To fit, their owners are
A hearsay of shapes, a bag
At these elbows, a button
Gone from this tight collar.
I think of all the feet
That walked in these shoes,
Toes down-pointing now from
A rail, each rail-held heel,
And each scuffed toe, caught in
The second-hand quadrille.
The strict proprietrix
Flicks ash on the bare floor.
The boards are a brushed dirt.
Even these women look
As taken off as shirts,
Worn sweaters, skirts, sea-boots,
And thrown down on a floor.
Coats, ranked on their hangers,
Pose—shamed vagrants, slaves
Whose prices she calls out
As you shuffle their shrugs.
And here a man may buy
One cufflink, scarves, or socks,

A glove, or soup-stained tie,
Or a large box of dust.
There could have been a war
Yesterday. I walk home,
A suitably ashamed
Observer of the poor;
And I wonder at the coins
On her watery tray,
By her pot-plants. What does
She wish for, having stood
So long by the red bars
Of her electric fire
In her shop, having seen
The fact of poverty
And served its enterprise
In England, arms folded,
Witnessing its shame,
Its sizes, dignity,
The hard, proud faces of
Regular customers,
Who buy, sell, delve into
Her tubs of washed-out thread?
A shabby drunk goes down
In a corner puddle.
When I got home, I crawled
Into my mouth, sat down,
And fell into a cloth sleep.
There's nothing to be done
Save follow the lost shoes.

Remembering Lunch

Noticing from what they talk about, and how they stand, or
                                                                    walk,
That my friends have lost the ability or inclination to wander
Along the shores of an estuary or sea in contented solitude,
Disturbs me on the increasingly tedious subject of myself.
I long for more chances to walk along depopulated shores,
For more hours dedicated to fine discriminations of mud
As it shades from grey to silver or dries into soft pottery;
Discriminations of wind, sky, rough grasses and water-birds,
And, above all, to be well-dressed in tweeds and serviceable
                                                                    shoes
Although not like an inverted popinjay of the demented gentry
But as a schoolmaster of some reading and sensibility
Circa 1930 and up to his eccentric week-end pursuits, noticing,
Before the flood of specialists, the trace of lost peoples
In a partly eroded mound, marks in the earth, or this and that
Turned over with the aforementioned impermeable footwear.
Describing this to my strangely sophisticated companions
Is to observe them docket it for future reference in
A pigeon-hole of the mind labelled *Possible Satires*.
We are far gone in our own decay. I admit it freely,
Longing no more for even the wherewithal of decent
                                                                    sufficiency
Or whatever hypothetical brilliance makes it possible.
Whatever my friends long for, they no longer confess it
In the afternoon twilight of a long lunch in London
After that moment when the last carafe has been ordered.
Such delicate conversations of years gone by! You would think
Perceptions of this sort best left for approaching senility,
Especially as, in my case, I was not born ever to expect

To enjoy so long-drawn-out a lunchtime at steep prices
Among tolerant waiters resigned to our lasting presences
As if they sense a recapitulation by young men of young men
In that fine hour of Edwardian promise at the *Tour Eiffel*
Or expatriate Americans and Irishmen in 'twenties Paris.
It is pretty well standard among literary phenomena.
Whether in the Rome of Marcus Martialis or London
                                           ordinaries
Favoured by roaring playwrights and poets destined for
Future righteousness or a destructive addiction to sack,
Lunch, lunch is a unitary principle, as Balzac would tell you
And as any man of letters consulting his watch towards noon
Would undoubtedly endorse. Lunch is the business of capitals,
Whether in *L'Escargot Bienvenue*, *Gobbles*, or the cheap Italian
                                            joint.
Impoverished or priggish in the provinces, where talent is born,
The angry poets look towards London as to a sea of restaurants,
Cursing the overpriced establishments of where they live
And the small scatter of the like-minded not on speaking
                                            terms.
But even this pleasure has waned, and its sum of parts—
People shaking hands on the pavement, a couple entering
A taxi hailed in the London rain, the red tears on a bottle
And the absorbing conspiracies and asserted judgements
Of young men in the self-confident flush of their promise—
Its sum of parts no longer presents a street of epiphanies.
Too much now has been spoken, or published, or unpublished.
Manias without charm, cynicism without wit, and integrity
Lying around so long it has begun to stink, can be seen and
                                            heard.
To come down south from the country in a freshly pressed
                                            suit
Is no longer the exercise in youthful if gauche dignity
It was once in days of innocent enthusiasm without routine.
And so I look forward to my tweed-clad solitude, alone

Beside a widening estuary, the lighthoused island appearing
Where waves of the sea turmoil against the river's waters
Baring their salty teeth and roaring. And here I can stand—
Forgive me my fantasies as, Lord, I surely forgive you yours—
In a pretence of being a John Buchan of the underdog,
With my waistcoated breast puffed against the wind. What do
                                                they long for?
Propping up bars with them I can pretend to be as they are
Though I no longer know what they are thinking, if ever I
                                                did,
And, raising this civil if not entirely sympathetic interest
In what they feel, I know it contributes little to them,
Adding, as it does, to a change in myself they might not notice,
Causing me this pain as I realize the way I must change
Is to be different from friends I love and whose company—
When the last carafe was ordered, an outrageous remark
                                                spoken,
Or someone announced his plan for an innovating stanza
Or a new development in his crowded sex-life—whose
                                                company
Was a landmark in my paltry accumulation of knowledge.
Perhaps, after all, this not altogether satisfactory
Independence of mind and identity before larger notions
Is a better mess to be in, with a pocketful of bread and cheese,
My hipflask and the *Poésie* of Philippe Jaccottet,
Listening to the sea compose its urbane wilderness,
Although it is a cause for fear to notice that only my footprints
Litter this deserted beach with signs of human approach,
Each squelch of leather on mud complaining, *But where are you
                                                going?*

Green Breeks

J. G. Lockhart, Memoirs of Sir Walter Scott, *Macmillan, 1900. Vol. 1,
pages 81–5.*

Crosscauseway, Bristo Street, and Potterrow,
In Edinburgh, seventeen eighty-three—
    Boys there were poor, their social class was 'low';
    Their futures lay in work or livery.
Sir Walter Scott says they 'inhabited'
These streets they lived on; but, in George's Square,
    'The author's father'—so Sir Walter said—
    Did not 'inhabit' but 'resided' there.
Young Walter and his chums were organized
Into a 'company' or 'regiment'.
    A 'lady of distinction', who despised
    The ragged street-boys from the tenements,
Gave Scott 'a handsome set of colours', which
Made Walter grateful to that Highland bitch
Who'd later 'clear' her kinsmen from her land,
That Duchess-Countess named for Sutherland.

From Potterrow, Crosscauseway, Bristo Street,
The poor boys came to 'bicker' on the Square—
    A military game, if indiscreet—
    To thrash the sons of those 'residing' there.
Offspring of State, Law, Ministry and Bank,
With flag aloft, defended their regime
    Against those 'chiefly of the lower rank',
    Boy-battles at a simplified extreme.
Though vanquished from the subtly written book
That's history, the street-boys often won—
    Scott says they did. Sir Walter undertook
    Average lies in how he wrote it down—

Mendacious annals—that no one should forget
When beggars win, they're in the horsemen's debt;
And only Scott has chronicled their war—
A beaten boy becomes the conqueror.

One of his enemies, says Scott, was both
Ajax and Achilles of the Crosscauseway—
    'The very picture of a youthful Goth'—
    The first to fight and last to run away.
Blue-eyed, with long fair hair, tall, finely made,
That boy-barbarian awed him. Scott could tell
    He and his class-mates mustered to degrade
    This brave, presumptious, vulgar general.
They called him Green Breeks, this boy whom Scott preserved
As a memento of his opposite
    That, cheating him of what he led and served,
    A novelist could have his way with it.
Scott draws the colour of his hero's eyes,
His shape, his height, but not the boy, who dies
    Within the pickle of Scott's quickened prose,
    Half-loved by Scott, half-feared, born to oppose.

In one fight, Green Breeks laid his hands upon
Sutherland's 'patrician standard'. Before
    He'd time to win it, he was faced with one
    Too zealous for 'the honour of the Corps'
Who had a hanger or *couteau de chasse*.
For honour, then, that boy cut Green Breeks down.
    To save a flag, the honour of his class,
    He struck him on the head and cut him down.
Imagined horsemen of the old regime
Transformed young Green Breeks to a Dying Gaul—
    A pictured history, the bronze of dream,

A classic gesture in an urban brawl.
Scott's friend disgraced his 'regiment' and showed
Expedient dragoonship was its code.
Where was nobility? But Scott, you found
Your life's obsession on that cobbled ground.

Scott turned our country round upon its name
And time. Its history obeyed his whip
        When Scott sent out his characters to claim
        Their pedigrees in Green Breeks' leadership.
I do not understand, Scott, what you meant
By your displaced verse-prose 'nobility'
        Unless the tatters of your 'regiment'
        Were patched on Green Breeks, that, for chivalry,
Your heroes might go forth and look the part—
Part man, part prince, part soldier and part God—
        Ridiculous and lacking in support
        As, when they fall, mere modern men applaud.
But Scott, you failed; for where your Green Breeks lives
Is that dark tenement of fugitives
Who, fled from time, have no need to endure
The quicklime of your ordered literature.

Green Breeks did not inform. He kept his pride.
He nursed his lovely grudge and sword-cracked skull
        And took both pain and bribery in his stride.
        They offered cash, 'smart money', to annul
Shame and dishonoured laws. He would not sell
His wound: let them remember it. Scott says
        That childish purse was small—part comical,
        Part serious: the whole antithesis.
They would not meet him face to face, but stood
On dignity and used a go-between,

Like states, transacting with the multitude,
    Who can negotiate, then intervene
With laws, with cavalry and troops, with style,
With system, representatives and guile,
Who, pompously, can compromise to win,
Pitch coins against a ragged ostentation.

Peasant baroque, like this, its nuts screwed tight
In praise of rabbles and those *sans culottes*,
    Won't change a thing. It whets an appetite,
    Unfankling truths inwoven like a knot.
It gestures like a ghost towards a ghost,
And, bringing Green Breeks back, or trying to,
    It reckons with desire, the human cost
    In losing what was old, and fierce, and true.
What did he do? Where did he live, and die?
That life can be imagined. I let him *be*.
    He is my light, conspirator and spy.
    He is perpetual. He is my country.
He is my people's minds, when they perceive
A native truth persisting in the weave
Of shabby happenings. When they turn their cheeks
The other way, he turns them back, my Green Breeks.

Green Breeks accepted what he asked them give—
A pound of snuff for 'some old woman—aunt,
    Grandmother, or the like,' with whom he lived.
    Kindness, like courtesy, must ever haunt
Love-raddled reminiscence, Walter Scott.
You cannot hide behind mock-epic prose
    Your love of 'haves', amusement at 'have-nots'.
    Between your lines, it's easy to suppose
Deeper affections generate each word

Recalling Green Breeks in your years of fame.
    You drank toasts to his name in Abbotsford,
        Proposed to Green Breeks, not his father's name.
Be not amused, Scott. Go, and give him thanks
He let you patronize his 'lower ranks'.
Go, talk to him, and tell him who you are,
Face to face, at last, Scott; and kiss his scar.

Tannahill

Robert Tannahill, 1774–1810

'I would I were a weaver, I could sing all manner of songs.'
Shakespeare

Aye, Bobbie Tannahill, I'll brew
Unhappy truths of verse and you
In Scots lines of the turn and screw.
    Aye, Tannahill,
This reckoning is overdue,
      Lamentable.

We sang your songs in Paisley's school,
Ink-fingered Dux and classroom fool,
Each little lord of ridicule;
    Aye, Tannahill,
All learned your sweet and bountiful
      Melodic drill.

By singing you, I understood
That poetry's lax brotherhood
Lived in my town; and it was good—
    Aye, Tannahill—
To learn that verse did not exclude
      A local skill.

Blackboyds and yeltrins in the year
Seventeen hundred and seventy-four
Were ripe and brilliant, born to dare
    'The sin of rhyme'
That Burns committed in his pure
      Intimate crime.

In seventeen hundred and eighty-six
They set you learn a weaver's tricks
While Burns discovered Muses vex
        As well as grace,
Young Burns, whose Scots proprietrix
        Spat in his face.

Douce dandies of the posh salons
Took that man in, as if on loan,
Then having raised, they laid him down,
        Their ploughman poet.
They made Society's decision,
        And let him know it.

Burns, Tannahill and Fergusson,
These jorum-jirgers, they could hone
A merry R, lick till they shone
        Gently stroked Ls,
And then die young, or in Darien,
        Ink's asphodels.

Young dead like Leyden, Smith and Gray,
Unread, forgotten, sternly weigh
Against the doors of elegy
        And find them shut.
Timor mortis conturbat me—
        Not to forget.

An antiquarian of old airs,
You played your flute at Renfrew's fairs;
You sang of amorous despairs
        And country courting.
Aye, Tannahill, hurt love confers
        A sweeter singing.

Composing verses at your bench,
Lines woven inch by linen inch
To follow each iambic hunch
     Into its art,
You sang, like a beginning finch,
     Your common heart.

A wabster's craft would teach a man
To live with art as an artisan.
As you could weave, teach me to scan
     And turn a rhyme,
Fraternally, like Caliban
     His low sublime.

When Paisley's bodies sought to learn
At the Star Inn and the Sun Tavern,
You, Tannahill, taught them discern
     False verse from true.
They 'kenned y'r faither', and would turn
     Their wits on you.

Once set in print, that was enough;
Your melodies had had their puff,
Their papery chance. With each rebuff
     Your inkwells dried;
You, Tannahill, in local chaff,
     Were vilified.

My Tannahill, the delicate
Delight of poetry is to wait
And, suffering the alphabet,
     Allow songs come
The way a prodigal in debt
     Walks slowly home.

You could not wait, yet overheard
A fame that rarely is conferred—
Anonymously choristered,
	A song you wrote;
A farm-girl, singing as she sheared,
	Your song, her throat.

And still they are singing, by Gryfe,
By Cart, with gentle disbelief
In the lilt of words against life;
	And your words breathe
In the pianos, with a little laugh,
	Keeping their faith.

Gone, gone down, with a song, gone down,
My Tannahill. The tavern town
Said one book was your last and frowned.
	The River Cart
Ran deep and waste where you would drown,
	Your counterpart.

You clutched the papers of your tongue:
Gone, gone down, gone down with a song.
Pity the mad, darkened with wrong.
	Home Lycidas,
You died in the dish-cloth Cart, among
	The ugliness.

And in the morning schoolboys came
To fish for papers, speak your name
And take their landed catches home,
	Dried on the gorse;
Aye, Tannahill, boys caught your poems,
	Lost, watery verse.

By broom, by briar, by Craigie Wood,
Through Cart-side's river neighbourhood,
Your papers rotting on the mud,
  My Tannahill!
But the shelfie and the hawthorn bud
  You could not kill.

John Wilson in Greenock, 1786

That day I stood before our magistrates
And minister, I hushed my heart's debates
With words and scenery, for I agreed
To let these pious dumplings intercede
Against my heard-of and once-printed *Clyde*
Which they thought damned, and I thought sanctified
Sights I had seen of water, wood and stone.
They took me, for I promised to abandon
'The profane and unprofitable art'
Of poetry. Swans sail, kingfishers dart
In colours of the fourteen halcyon days:
To think of them engenders miseries
In this man bonded to his self-disgust.
I read my *Clyde* as an unwritten ghost.

I dreamt of living by the breath of fame,
A matter most opprobrious to them
Who pay me govern, according to their rule,
The wastrel brats of Greenock's Grammar School.
For the sake of my family, I waste
What I once loved, and hope to see disgraced
My living mind, which, for a stipend, closed
Itself on life and what life once proposed
Along the river-banks I loved and walked—
My classic verse shut tight, my heart unlocked.
What can I do but curse this pen, this hand
That's paid to cultivate the sterile sand
Of worthless juveniles? They know me for
My whipping tawse, and as ambassador
From fantasy, where I, their Master, write
Five-beat iambic artifice, contrite
No more, high-placed and able to afford

The only breaking of my written word
It would not break my heart to break—my name,
Myself. John Wilson, Master, will reclaim
John Wilson, poet, his being and his soul,
From contracts binding him to the control
Of ministers and moralists whose teeth,
He hopes, will fester in their Godly breath
And, rotted on their speech, will fall, to skid
Beneath the brogues of others *unco guid*.

By Nethan's banks, I first took up my pen
To lift our Lowland snipe and water-hen
Into Arcadia from Lanarkshire.
I walked them all, Gryfe, Cart and Douglas Water,
By Avon, Calder and by Elvan-Clyde
Where my half-tutored art was fortified
By waterfalls where Clyde is young and free,
As I was then, in that complicity
Clyde worked with verse. This was the way of it,
That I, John Wilson, Master, scholar, poet,
Would come to sign my name in hunger on
Vouchsafements of my own obscure damnation.

A nobleman, whom I beseeched, was pleased
To praise my poem, and see my troubles eased.
But then he died, before he could convert
His word to what I needed most, a shirt,
One pair of breeks, a bench, and pen and ink,
A room near water, and sweet time to think.
He tried, in jest, with guns, to frighten me,
Testing my courage or tenacity;
And what I swallowed then did me no good
As, penniless, I tasted livelihood,
Salt on my tongue, and sweat within my throat,
My life reduced to future anecdote.

In several mishandled interviews
I talked my gifts away, while their abuse,

To me, and poetry, earned me my bread,
Which I was glad of, for, a table, spread
Before a wife and children, is not greed,
And, knowing love, is somehow to succeed,
At least at home. Therefore, I dropped my pen
To teach Latinity in Rutherglen,
For what it was worth. I was disguised.
Each night I dreamt of fame as I revised
My praised and printed *Clyde*. I paid my rent
On every week of that imprisonment.
I paid my way, but what I could not buy
Was time enough to work and versify
The river of my mind into its soul,
Its pure alluded water, pool and fall,
Through birkenshaw, past steadings, with the grace
A classic metre grafts on native place.
For this, crude kirkmen treat me to contempt.
They do not know the harmony I dreamt
In days of promises I could not keep.
Too many obstacles, the rivers deep—
I could not climb or cross, but slaved instead
To see my wife, myself, my children fed.
Too many patriarchs and ministers
Between my Muse and me, that rose of hers
Soon crushed beneath the booted patriarchs—
A Renfrew rose, an Ayrshire rose, or Lanark's.
Wild rose and briar, tormentil and broom,
I see you through a coward's nom-de-plume,
And make this promise now, that once again
I'll draw you on the metres of my pen
To beats of which I dandle my own true
Love-children on the days I think of you.
Dear rivers, know, and see, your poet nurse
His children on his love's pentameters.
　　　That men with leisure, brave, or cunning, wise

Or ruthless men, might make the sacrifice
Is why I write this now, to take my chance
They'll blame my misdemeanours on finance
But note my tears, and know I broke my heart
For this profane, unprofitable art.
I see a rose, but am forbidden it.
I see a swan, but must not mention it.
I see a ruin, but I must not confer
Discarded history with music's whirr.
I see a stream, but I must not discern
A heathen Georgic in a Lowland burn.
Come, pity my embezzled universe,
My thwarted bestiary and guilty purse
As, high up on Greenock at the windy jaws
I hear again the literate applause
Of Elvan Water chattering to me
Its small-talk of polite society;
Or Cora Linn, in its delicious spate,
Delinquent, plunging and importunate.
A life ago I saw in Cadzow's bull
Europa and the Thunderer annul
The moral average, and once I saw
Naiads at Lanark, where the birkenshaw
Throws shadows on a water that acclaims
These pagan ladies at their water-games.
And one has come to us from Ayrshire's sod
Who jests at Kirks and outmanoeuvres God.
So tell them this, them, and their kind who set
My bond and oath before me, the alphabet
They cannot thole to hear as melody
Will do them down as sure as they downed me
Unless they learn a way of blotting truth
And shut his mouth, and shut his singing mouth
As they imprisoned mine, and dispossess
His art with purchased righteousness.

Buy and subvert that wanton, better man,
Profane, unprofitable citizen!
　　　With teaching—wed, my fame and art cut short;
With bitterness and nine bairns to support—
I earn my bread, a fugitive from song
Who measures wordless verses on his tongue
And keeps his word. I walk into the night
With beer and brandy for my appetite
Pretending my dismantled Muse deplored
The leisure which my purse could not afford.
From my mistakes and harbour tavern grog
I count my country in a catalogue
Of native vomits at the Clyde's sick mouth
Where brutish skippers mock me for my truth.
What consolation is it, what amends,
I live now where my mighty river ends?
Salt wilderness erupts from pastorals
At this Hesperides, and the sky falls
Where ocean's mercantile and cold Firth-tide
Confronts the country waters from the Clyde?
　　　I suffer wordlessly, as if the King
Or Ministers of State forbade me sing;
As if by seeming far from God and thrift
There was a blameless treason in my gift.
Those who come after me, whose mouths are shut,
Abandon tricks of *if*, *perhaps* and *but*,
And sign no bonds, but claim that *to be free*
Is carried on the back of poetry.
Blame me, if you must blame me; and say my will
Was feeble-weak, and then contemptible;
That in the theatres of verse, my *Clyde*
Draws no applause. But know, I worked, and tried;
And hope still for a small posterity
And, through a chink in time, to hear men say,
That, wasting these best talents of my life,
I fed my children and I loved my wife.

Valerio

A poem-film, starring Anthony Quinn

Valerio gets down from his mule.
He holds a leather lung to his mouth.
It is the wine of his country.
As he drinks it, he looks down on
A valley that was seldom green
In the days when he, too, dug and hoe'd.
It was the Irrigation Project
Delivered this green outlook.
For years they demanded such a thing.
Five years ago, the government
Turned up and turned on water.
Men went to jail in 1928,
Demanding water and a few pipes.
Men went to jail in '32,
After two men died in the scuffle.
What were their names? Brave men, anyway . . .
Priests don't like Valerio.
Who *does* like him? Nobody does.
He bawls insults at the lawyer.
'Your feet', he yells, 'disturb the dust
And spiderwebs of fascism!'
Everybody laughs at him.
He insults the wife of the mayor.
'Your father sent men to their deaths!'
'Why don't you forget, Valerio?
Why don't you forgive and forget?'
Valerio walks away, tugging
His mule on its halter, grunting.
'And why did he never marry, eh?'
He tows his mule into the village

Surrounded now by new houses.
By a wall he can hear young bathers
In the swimming-pool of the hotel.
There's nothing for him at the Post Office.
Valerio, who led the partisans,
There's no letter for Valerio.
He walks out of a page of
Silone's early stories, sunlight
Redesigning the dust from the building-site.
'Who'd write to *him*?' everybody asks.
'Can he even *read*?' 'They say he fought
Two years in the hills, up there.'
A young man watches him go by
Then takes a seat with an open view.
He sees Valerio climb the old track.
'They say he still lives up there,'
Says his uncle. 'It's a sad story.
Personally, I preferred to survive.'
Valerio sits on a boulder
And looks at yellow earth-movers
Nudge and butt at the landscape
In which, for years, he lay concealed.
He goes higher, and farther away.
The young man watching him turns
To look at a girl on a bicycle.
When he turns back, Valerio's gone.
He doesn't know why, but a tear
Drips down the young man's cheek, and falls
Into the dust, where, soon, it dries.
It was over there, by the sluice
Of the Irrigation Project
Valerio ran with a girl
That night when everything went wrong.
Demented Germans were burning farms,
Burning everything they couldn't eat

Or take with them, and the sky heaved
In illuminated rumbles.
And he had six bullets left
Out of the twelve he had to start with.
Six times he'd missed, and ten friends dead.
If only one had lived! Just one.
Even the Englishman who'd come
Out of the sky by parachute
With his bad Italian, his promises,
And who was shot jumping the dry stream-bed.
Who ever heard of such a thing—
A dead, long-jumping Englishman?
If he had lived, Valerio thinks,
Then he, at least, would write to me.
Valerio lost a boot and breath.
There was a noise where there should have been none.
She sighed. Her grip was tight.
A minute went by and then she fell.
He didn't even know her name, not then,
Not now, a courier from somewhere.
Fear and courage without a name!
The dead, anonymous as furniture . . .
He hid and waited for two Germans,
Who tapped her body with their boots,
Then turned her over, tearing off
Her covert crucifix.
He's seen so much of his country
Through rifle-sights. Now, as he looks,
He sees the German metal shine,
Not quite reflections, but more like
Reflections in disguise, dull light.
Two shots towards the metal.
A door bangs in the village and
He twists the halter which he drags his mule by.
He carried the girl into the hills
And buried her at dawn beside

The spring, where goats drink. Their bells,
He was told, as a child, inspired
A poet from Rome to write a sonnet.
Since then, he dreams of lovers
With bells around their throats,
And, cradled in his palm, his warm
And miniature Christ still suffers.
Only Valerio knows, his lips on the water,
His knees among picnic litter.
Whenever he remembers her
He looks at his four bullets with
The agony of Christ—one for
The lawyer, and one for the lawyer's wife;
One for the lawyer's father who
Was worse than his fat son; one for
The priest. The man in the Post Office
Who claims he has had no letter
Will be taken care of with a knife.
Valerio puts the lung of wine
To his mouth that has not kissed
His mouth shut tight on a secret
A mouth which refuses to speak
A mouth which gave up cursing years ago
A mouth which mumbles when drunk
A mouth wise in wine and water
A mouth which chokes on its insults.
Foreign tourists have rented the summer.
Valerio does not know why
They are responsible—he scans
The car-park through German binoculars—
All he knows is that they are.
And he, Valerio, is honoured in that country,
And in other countries where
They clench their fists for Valerio
Without knowing the name of Valerio.
He counts his bullets. He guards his spring.

La Route

A poem-film, starring Jean-Paul Belmondo

Whether or not the man driving
Is really my chauffeur—he is
A pal who happens to like caps—
Is unlikely, at this speed, to
Bother anyone we pass on
These country roads.
           This is the speed
We go at: illegible notices,
A gate half-open to a lane
Where . . . Hand on a shutter that's . . .
Someone's jumping off a tower
On a château that's blinked by sun.
No. It's a child who's throwing
Newspapers out of a window.
Is it? Why is he doing that?
Swift dapples of lime-shade are
Left behind, cool places for *boule*,
Old men who shuffle in the dust.
A silent weir; a fisherman
Snapped in the frame of pouring out
His glugless wine . . .
           And in here it's
Smoke, which has no words, despite mouths
Blowing it out; and no one wonders
Out there in the houses, up there
In the villas which have survived
The holidays and good times of
Their smart owners, that inside here
Is a man sitting on the back-seat
Notorious for fifty crimes,

For whom old peasant women in
Their hats are a multitude of
His own mother and several aunts;
Or that the young men in cafés—
Blurred, talking—are as fragile straws
He wishes he could catch with his eyes.
For I need to be one of them
Again, and stripped entirely clean
Of infidelity, this silk,
This speed and all that I have done.
These obsolete advertisements,
Each populated hole in the shade . . .
And it is not anonymous
Even at this speed which can make
A cigarette seem longer, or
The radio a function of
Travelling, a voice of nowhere
And no one at a microphone.
The seat's leather is heating up;
An open book is fast asleep.
She has left her hairbrush. It is
Rocking gently in a corner of
The hot back-seat. To take it back
Would not be gallantry, but
A waste of petrol. So why did
She choose to remain there, with them?
Nadine . . . Ruthless and beautiful:
She looks like both ideals. It is
A better trip without her; she, she . . .
How many women have I known?
If only, Nadine, you were not a liar . . .
That boy in the nylon overalls
Who is . . . that little bridge; these trees;
These children on stilts. She would have
Turned the radio up, too loud,

And chattered like the tart she was,
A fishwife slimmed for luxury,
A swimming-pool girl, a girl made by
Advertisements, my kind of girl
Who tastes of other men's champagne.
I doze like an open book, open,
Where my real life is written, told,
Told and shown, lying in two halves
And hinged, so, like the door I did
Not go through; and I think I am
A man who had no mother, who,
Therefore, is bad, and going to
A city where Max is standing
In a doorway, thinking that life
Is a dandy with a flick-knife
And a certain self-confidence
In clever cuts with it—up-cut,
Into the belly, and throat-cut,
For the kill. He thinks I don't know.
I know who paid him kill you, Jean.
I know he told you it was me,
But it wasn't, and you knew it.
Why, friend, do I weaken before
This dutiful revenge, as if
I've had enough, and this the last?
We are passing the houses of
Doctors and Professors. Sight
Is not what it was on this journey.
Max I see more clearly as
An executioner, or, if
Not that, then, at least, destiny
Who stands well-dressed in a shadow;
And faces, certainly, are not
So beautiful, nor are gardens
Anything like what I have seen

Today, with all the little quirks
People share, twitches, quarrels, food,
Their affections, their crazed sweetness
Accusing me. So, it is true:
There is a deep hole in the world.
Friend, you were with me, under the trees,
That summer we decided to reap
The pious franc instead of hay.
We did it with laughter. We were *good*.
It's a long road back; there were thefts
Conducted in the name of Law
Everywhere along it, making me
Almost a good man, who, sunk
In the ghost of my personality
Cannot remember my last drink
Or when I lit this cigarette.
It could have been years ago
Before the multitudes of mothers.
'Try a schoolmistress. She'll mother you.'
You used to say that, Jean, teasing me.
I aged like a ballad, always young.
No matter what I did, or thought,
An innocence clung to me like
A skin, a lime-shade, or like hair:
A history of love and theft,
Those deals; a history of suits
And big tips left in restaurants,
The career of my machismo—
Never stuck for a dame, or lost
For introductions to the rich.
Why, Jean, do they like crooks so much
In France? What's wrong with honesty?
A long road, Jean, but I never met
Anyone like me; I never met
Myself among the handshakes.

Max, I am coming to get you,
But, you bastard, if you stick me
It will be just as well, for I
Have seen a big hole in the world
That's full of paymasters, and you,
And I know what you don't, which is
That I'll go back the way I came
As safely on this leather seat,
Unnoticed in a machine, driven
By a black-capped chauffeur who says
Nothing, who, whatever happens,
Either way, Max, will take me home,
Who will have the good sense to know
Where, in the country, that is.

The Gallery

See, how this lady rises on her swing
Encouraged by the brush of Fragonard,
As light as love, as ruthless as the Czar,
Who, from her height, looks down on everything.

When on a canvas an oil-eye of blue
Has tiny fissures, you can stand behind,
Imagine time, observe, and condescend,
Wink at and spit on those who are not you.

Out of the eye of Christ, you might see God;
Or, from your swing, see pastoral machines
Romanticized, re-made as guillotines;
Or, Goya's captive, face a firing-squad;

Or, Goya's soldier, be condemned to hear
Eternity in the museum of death—
Your moment after triggering—and with
The horror of aesthetics in your ears.

Ah, they were lucky, who were drawn from life
By river-banks in summer, in café scenes,
The way they were, for all their speechless pains,
That absinthe drinker and his sober wife.

The Deserter

Homage to Robert Desnos

'Somewhere in the world, at the foot of an embankment,
A deserter parleys with sentries who don't understand his language.'

At the world's end, just before everything stops,
There may not be a war going on, but it is where
Broken lines of contested frontiers converge,
Drawn long ago by the hands of shrewd statesmen
In the years when they bagged the knees and elbows of their suits
In the grandest of all the world's capital cities.

It is at this place they keep the railway carriages
Of armistice and treaties, those waggons which brought
The revolutionary and his bales of pamphlets.
Many cattle trucks rot on a spread of sidings
With their memories of last kisses, of goodbyes,
A child's hand in yours, his eyes under the skip of his cap.

This is the last mortuary, the bottom inch of six feet,
Home to pallid garrisons sustained on cigarettes
And fantasies of strangers, wrapped in greatcoats

The way the inflexible uphold their ideologies.
Their freezing breath fastens them as if by chains
To a heaven above the arc-lamps, above innocent airliners.

Snow has begun to fall on the guilty secrets of Europe.
Here, where the lines meet, and emplacements rise up
Out of mined earth in their laurels of wire, a man,
Unarmed, talks with another five who hold their guns
On him. This conversation is composed of cloth,
Of buttons, stars, and boots. Of wood. Of steel. Of wire.

*'A spectre in a well-tailored shroud
Smoked a cigar at the window of his apartment.'*

We have seen him, this upright father
Who has the stately manners of a priest,
Who, when he lets it slip, behaves like a tycoon
In armaments, believing that they died
In Buchenwald for capitalism, for him.

We have dined with this stranger, talked at meat
With him after the funerals of our fathers.
Our wives are fond of him. They have been known to
Abscond to some Swiss chalet with him where
He keeps the instruments of pleasure.

How confidently the ash balances on
The tip of his cigar, a grey drool;
And with what contempt for his possessions
He lets it fall . . . . We have seen him in cafés,
Served, as if he has only to wave his hand.

We are asked to die for him, and we die.
In the unlikeliest places, we have died,
Places we never dreamt of sending postcards from.
There, in his red resorts, men vanish in
Factories that grind through men and native parishes.

Never to die, not even in the grand style
Tended by nieces married to Counts and Princes,
But to live always, at the concept of wealth,
In galleries and in the regularity of verse,
In metronomes pledged to custom,

And in the regulation of wages and bread,
Never to die. O with how much passion
We can condemn this man many have died for.
He claims even to love nature.
He praises its brutality as he hunts.

In his mouth is the taste of Europe,
Its rank saliva. When I see this ghost,
I am afraid of him, who, from his window,
Spits on the lives of so many people,
On my mother, my father, my wife, my friends, myself.

'*A widow in her wedding-gown gets into the wrong train.*'

So much is average, so much
That anyone can buy or touch,
Things you can watch, or put to sleep,
That walk, or run on wheels, or creep.

Other things are just mistaken,
Marriages, or wrong trains taken.
A widow in her wedding-gown
Alights somewhere, in the wrong town.

O Lady, run, it's over now,
Whatever grief that marked your brow
With something like a brilliant star
To tell this city who you are.

I shall possess your soul, bereaved
Of everything for which it lived.
I am a specialist of tears.
I weep the world's, let me weep yours.

I listen to the song you sing
About two lives, two wedding-rings.
I listen as you fold your dress
To the mute curves of your nakedness.

Lamp-posts

You find them in the cities of Europe,
Ornate plush iron, stooped, fluted, winged,
And in the postures of old *boulevardiers*.
They stand outside hotels and embassies
As the commissionaires of *savoir faire*
And architecture, dressed in an era
Along the fashionable avenues.
In Paris like the ghosts of Baudelaire,
And in Prague like a street of Kafkas,
They contemplate the shadows round their feet.
Throw them a coin or two, for they are beggars
Touting beneath electric epaulettes
For the recovery of time, for hooves,
For carriages and footmen, or for her
Habsburgian slipper fallen in a pulse
Of gas-light and an equerry kneeling
To fit the slipper to its royal foot.
The rehabilitated lamps of Warsaw
Have been hung with civilians, improvised
As gallows while the multitudes of death
Marched over the rubble, in the darkness.
Therefore I mourn these uprooted lamp-posts
That lean against a wall, in a corner of
This warehouse, bleak, municipal, leaning
In stances of exhaustion, their arms across
Their eyes, their brows against a bare brick wall.

The Miniature Métro

I walked over the changed fields of Inchinnan
With Arthur Rimbaud and a half of Bells.
Bulldozers were prehistoric and yellow
Resting on their shovels inside the hill
They had opened up like archeologists.
Never had I seen deeper into the earth
Than to the depths of a plough's blade
Or deeper than the depth of drain-layers
Though silver trowels of my imagination dug
A minature Métro, looping the parish
Under the farms of Port Nauld and Freelands,
Flourish, Town of Inchinnan and Birgaraw.
'Horses! Marvellous large horses!' I shouted,
In a gesture of whisky's rhetoric.
So I told him my philosophy of departures
In which are regretted leave-takings of things,
People, and the summers of years gone by
According to a rule of random timetables.
Even places can become unobtainable.
'There are no departures,' Arthur said.
'In the spirit there is neither profit or loss
And in imagination there are no shortages
While its abundances are illusory.
Confront your despair with enthusiasm.'
But I wasn't listening and I changed the subject.
'A plough is what I drive on my typewriter,
Though that is to imitate an Irish friend
Who lifts his pen and says he'll dig with it.
I click-click to my equine keyboard,
Giddying-up the alphabet and hyphens.

77

I coax the semi-colons with the Horseman's Word.'
There was a long silence where we stood among
Grease-proofed lunch-wrappers of the operatives
Before a scraped cliff of clay and muds, watching
Strata where roots end, deeper earth begins
Its absence of relics—pure mineral.
'*Dig* with it?' asked Arthur Rimbaud. '*Giddy-up?*
Now are the peasant singers of yesteryear
Orthodox naturalists of the work ethic.'
'Oh,' I said, 'but you wrote once, The hand
That holds the pen's the hand that holds the plough.
There nature and the modern shake hands together.'
'I never heard a peasant yet,' said Arthur,
'—And pass me that bottle—acknowledge pen
And plough in the one breath, except for laughs.
As for work, they can force you to do it.
Dig with it? Tell that man he's better off
With his pen in his ear or up his arse.
There are no pleasures in the laws of work,
Which do no good, nor can they make you free.'
But I wrote this on my horse-writer.
Old ways die hard, or do not die at all.

Loch Music

I listen as recorded Bach
Restates the rhythms of a loch.
Through blends of dusk and dragonflies
A music settles on my eyes
Until I hear the living moors,
Sunk stones and shadowed conifers,
And what I hear is what I see,
A summer night's divinity.
And I am not administered
Tonight, but feel my life transferred
Beyond the realm of where I am
Into a personal extreme,
As on my wrist, my eager pulse
Counts out the blood of someone else.
Mist-moving trees proclaim a sense
Of sight without intelligence;
The intellects of water teach
A truth that's physical and rich.
I nourish nothing with the stars,
With minerals, as I disperse,
A scattering of quavered wash
As light against the wind as ash.

Fallen among anti-Semites

With thirst quenched on this wine,
My tongue sits in its mouth
Immersed in reddened saliva—
A man in a bath of blood.

Wednesday

For Plato and for Mrs MacAvoy
At Number 18, I dedicate this sheet
Of paper I am writing on, on which,
While pondering it, I see have fallen
Sleep from my eyes, a crumb of cake,
A small flake from the scab on my nose
That has been bothering me all week.
To Heinrich Böll, for his short stories,
I scratch my pen across a sheet of paper.
With ink which stores the lovely alphabet
I draw a map of pleasure on this snow.
It is like filling in a form, this life.
I do not like my milkman, but I like
His milk-float's whispers on our leafy street.
For Albert Camus, who, alas, is dead,
I notice that a hair adorns this paper,
A hair from my moustache, and, for some reason—
I do not know what it is doing here—
The small pool of a tear,
Slowly absorbing its own curvature.

Ode to a Paperclip

When I speak to you, paperclip, urging you
To get a move on and metamorphose,
You sit there mating with the light that shines
Out of your minerals, a brighter glint
Where, rounding at a loop, you meet the sun.
Paperclip, I like you, I need you.
Please, turn into something wonderful.

    I remember restless clerks, in boring places,
Unbend you to caress their ears, tickling
Their lobes, or, slowly, linking you until
They forged one of their office necklaces—
A daisy-chain, from flowers of the desk;
Or straighten you, to dab at inky fluff
Mossed round a comma or an asterisk.

    You have more uses than your name pretends.
Intimately fingered all late afternoon,
Frustrations weave you into metal knots,
Boredom's insignia in the typing-pools.
A secretary, composed but fidgeting,
Was once chastised with airborne paperclips,
But no one noticed what was being thrown.

    A box of you, when brought up from the store,
Then opened, looked at, looks like dying sprats,
All life in its pathetic multiples.
But these are not your proper transformations.
Who knows what purpose you'll be made to serve
When a suspender is in deep crisis, or
The manager's braces tear his buttons off?

    It's you they think of first, because they know
Your versatility can be delivered

On bodice straps or snapped elastics.
It's your neutrality that gets me down—
Disarming. Why do you do it? You work
On dictats to the underlings of death
As readily as you fasten up the drafts
    A democrat compiles on human rights.
Good and/or bad, important/unimportant—
Little survivor, you go where you're sent,
On memoranda from the Chiefs of Staff
To Ministers of State, down to the note
A man finds clipped inside his wage packet,
Saying, *Sorry, you've been made redundant.*
    You also get lost and nobody cares.
It's part of your status to turn up in
A handful of change, or to appear from
Her handbag when she's powdering her nose.
You've no prestige at all, a tiny one
Among the commonplace, the vacuumed millions,
Diminished things, the meek disposables.
    Hand-made gold-plated paperclips do not,
I am sure of it, get made, let alone
Presented at executive goodbyes,
Although I've seen a breasty typist wear you
As earrings and, on her, you looked like treasure.
More than familiars, more than desk-top trinkets,
You're precious, though we may not choose to say so.
    Give them gold watches or cut-glass decanters,
It's you they're likely to remember as
The days go by, watched from their patios,
As, too, they think of Miss-What-Was-Her-Name—
Evasive, leggy and impertinent—
The one who worked gymnastic, sculptural
Designs in wire, her secretarial art.
    Ubiquitous, docile and mass-produced,
Existing in relationship to work

And tedium expressed thereof, you are
As functional as roads or pen and ink.
A box of you, when shaken on the ear,
Can make Brazilian noises, a rhythmic sea,
Plural as salt, as leaves, as citizens.

Ghost-bullets, triple-loops, no matter what
Inquiring minds might call your outline capsules,
You change your shapes and will go anywhere,
Do anything for a piece of the action.
Immoralist! Turncoat! Mercenary!
You don't need her, or him—Love me; love me,
And go where I go, gentle talisman.

Ratatouille

I

Consider, please, this dish of ratatouille.
Neither will it invade Afghanistan
Or boycott the Olympic Games in a huff.
It likes the paintings of Raoul Dufy.
It feeds the playboy and the working-man.
Of wine and sun it cannot get enough.
It has no enemies, no, not even
Salade niçoise or phoney recipes,
Not Leonid Brezhnev, no, not Ronald Reagan.
It is the fruits of earth, this ratatouille,
And it has many friends, including me.
Come, lovers of ratatouille, and unite!

II

It is a sort of dream, which coincides
With the pacific relaxations called
Preferred Reality. Men who forget
Lovingly chopped-up cloves of *ail*, who scorn
The job of slicing two good peppers thinly,
Then two large onions and six aubergines—
Those long, impassioned and imperial purples—
Which, with six courgettes, you sift with salt
And cover with a plate for one round hour;
Or men who do not care to know about
The eight ripe *pommes d'amour* their wives have need of,
Preparing ratatouille, who give no thought to
The cup of olive oil that's heated in

Their heaviest pan, or onions, fried with garlic
For five observant minutes, before they add
Aubergines, courgettes, peppers, tomatoes;
Or men who give no thought to what their wives
Are thinking as they stand beside their stoves
When seasoning is sprinkled on, before
A *bouquet garni* is dropped in—these men
Invade Afghanistan, boycott the Games,
Call off their fixtures and prepare for war.

III

Cook for one hour, and then serve hot or cold.
Eat it, for preference, under the sun,
But, if you are Northern, you may eat
Your ratatouille imagining Provence.
Believe me, it goes well with everything,
As love does, as peace does, as summers do
Or any other season, as a lifetime does.
Acquire, then, for yourselves, ingredients;
Prepare this stew of love, and ask for more.
Quick, before it is too late. *Bon appetit*!

Notes

Some Scottish words are glossed here. A few are obsolete, but used here for affection's sake. Others are written in spellings which match the way I speak them.

St. Kilda's Parliament
'hazelraw', lichen

The Apple Tree
'dailygone', dusk; 'sneddins', prunings, twigs; 'dailyday', commonplace, perpetual; 'whindlestrae', dead grass.

The Harp of Renfrewshire
The title of the poem is taken from that of an anthology published in Paisley, 1819. The map is from Johan Blaeu's *Atlas Novus*, 1654.
'darg', a day's work; 'brose', kinds of porridge, or any commonplace food; 'davoch', an ancient measurement of land.

Tannahill
'blackboyd', blackberry; 'yeltrin', the yellow-hammer; 'jorumjirger', a fiddler; 'Darien', the Edinburgh Baedlam; 'wabster', weaver; 'kenned y'r faither', knew your father: i.e. a put-down, on grounds of familiarity; 'shelfie', the chaffinch.

John Wilson in Greenock
Wilson's poem *Clyde* can be read in Leyden, *Scottish Descriptive Poems* (1803).
'birkenshaw', a birchwood